Dan Pats Nim

Written by Tina Pietron

Illustrated by Khama Lwanda

Collins

Nim taps Dan.

Dan sits.

4

Nim pats it.

Dan dips it in.

Nim sits.

Dan tips it.

Dan sips it.

Nim sits in. Pat, pat.

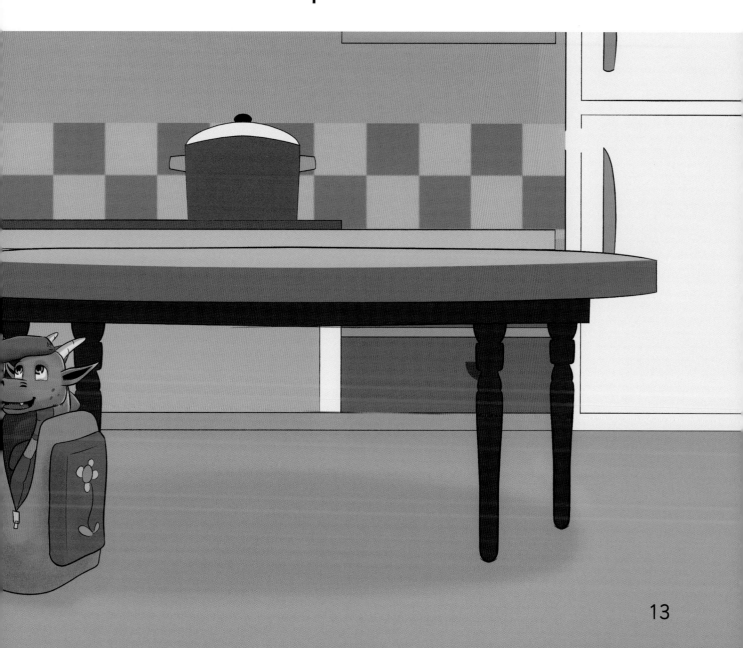

🐾 Review: After reading 🐾

Use your assessment from hearing the children read to choose any GPCs and words that need additional practice.

Read 1: Decoding

- Ensure the children can read words ending in "s" successfully. Ask the children to turn to pages 2–3. Show them how to read the word **taps** by covering up the "s" reading the word "tap" and then adding the "s" to read the whole word **taps**.
- On page 6, ask the children what Nim wants Dan to do. (e.g. *put the flannel in the water*) On page 7, ask: What does Dan do to **dip** his flannel? (e.g. *puts it in the water*)
- Turn to the "I spy" pages (14–15). Say: I can see lots of things that have the /d/ sound. Point to the dog and say "dog", emphasising the /d/ sound. Ask the children to find other things that contain the /d/ sound. (*duck, doll, doughnut, dragon, dolphin, dragonfly, dig, draw*)
- Point to the words on page 3. Ask: Can you blend in your head (silently) when you read these words aloud?

Read 2: Prosody

- Decide together on a type of voice for Nim, the dragon, and Dan the boy.
- Together, read the words on the left-hand pages, ensuring the children use the correct character voice.

Read 3: Comprehension

- Ask the children to describe or retell any stories they have read about pet dragons. Would they like a pet dragon? Why/Why not?
- Ask: What time of day is it? Do you do these things before you go to school, too?
- Encourage the children to retell the story, explaining what Dan and Nim did in the correct order. Ask:
  - What did Nim do first? (e.g. *woke up Dan*)
  - What did Nim and Dan do in the bathroom? (*Nim had a bath*; *Dan washed with a flannel*)
  - What happened at the end? (*Dan asked Nim to get in his school bag*)